Gadgets and Gizmos

Contents

Features

Why was Alfred Nobel upset about how people used his invention? Find out on page 5.

What in the world is a gizmo? Discover the answer on page 7.

Have you ever wondered how a roller coaster can go upside down without tipping out its passengers? Turn to **In a Spin** on page 14 and try the experiment.

Do you know robots can operate on people? See page 23 to find out more.

What was the first flying machine?

Visit **www.rigbyinfoquest.com**
for more about **FLIGHT.**

About Invention

An **invention** can change our world and make our lives easier, safer, faster, more interesting, or more fun. For thousands of years, people have been inventing things. When we switch on a computer, ride a bicycle, read a book, or zip up a jacket, we are using the work of inventors.

Inventors create new ideas, and ideas can lead to new inventions.

Alfred Nobel (1833–1896) was a scientist from Sweden who invented dynamite. He wanted his invention to be used in mines to make blasting rock safer. However, dynamite was used in wartime to kill and destroy. Alfred Nobel was very upset about this, so he used the money he made from his invention to set up special awards called Nobel Prizes. These are given every year to people who have done important and lasting things for science, writing, peace, and business.

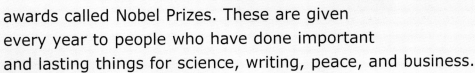

Figure It Out

An invention may be simple, like a button, or it may be made up of many parts, like a television. All inventions, however, use **scientific principles.** Inventors make use of these principles to invent new objects and improve the objects we already have. If we understand some of these principles, it is easier for us to figure out how machines and gadgets work.

Aerodynamics

Aerodynamics is about using the scientific principles of the forces caused by air as it flows around objects and pushes on them. Bicycle designs work by these principles. Today's bicycles are fast and strong.

Dandy horse
1790

Penny-farthing
1870

In 1886, a Frenchman named Mr. Gadget sold models of the Statue of Liberty to New York visitors in the United States. The people who bought these models called them gadgets. The word *gadget* has been used ever since to describe simple but clever machines or tools. The word *gizmo* is a made-up word that people use when they can't remember the name of an object.

Safety bike
1879

Aerodynamic bike
1980s

Principles of Things

Air Pressure
A drinking straw uses air pressure. When air is sucked out of a straw, the air pressure outside the straw is stronger and pushes the drink up.

Combustion
Combustion is a word for burning. It happens when something uses oxygen and gives off energy—often heat and light.

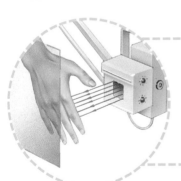

Electromagnetic Radiation
Electromagnetic radiation is electric and magnetic energy that moves through space together. An example of this is an x-ray.

Gravity
Gravity is the force that pulls everything toward the ground. An apple falls from a tree to the ground because of gravity.

Leverage

When something is pushed or lifted to move a heavy weight, it is using leverage. A wheelbarrow is one kind of lever.

Magnetism

Magnetism is the force of a magnet. A magnet attracts, or pulls, some metals such as steel. A magnetic force can also push magnets apart.

Reflection

When light hits a surface, it bounces like a ball. We can see ourselves in a mirror because light is reflected by the mirror.

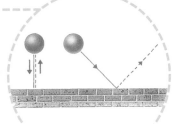

Refraction

Refraction is light bending as it passes through water or clear objects such as windows. White light is sometimes split into its seven colors.

Gravity pulls the roller coaster to the bottom of the track. Speed carries it forward and downward and makes it go faster. The curve of the track forces the roller coaster to move in loops. Although passengers feel like they are flying through air, the roller coaster is firmly on the track and the passengers are held tightly in their seats.

The car has wheels that are fastened to the track.

Fun and Thrills

People have invented many machines and games for fun and thrills. An amusement park is full of exciting rides and games that spin you, surprise you, and may even scare you! Many of these rides make use of gravity and speed. A roller coaster twists and turns, throwing its passengers from side to side. Sometimes it even turns upside down.

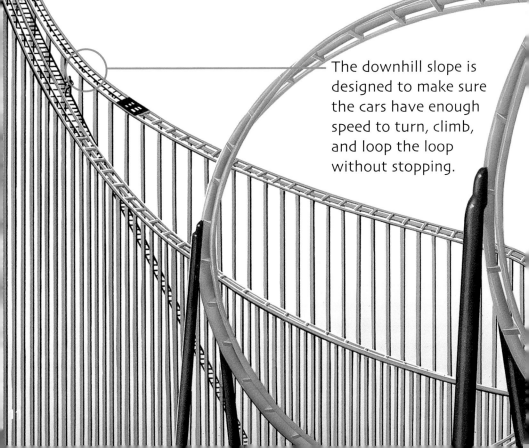

The downhill slope is designed to make sure the cars have enough speed to turn, climb, and loop the loop without stopping.

Science at Work

Scientific principles are put to use in everyday objects. Inventions such as safety pins use leverage action. The pins were perfect when they were first invented in 1849, and they have changed very little since. Other inventions, such as microwave ovens, are always being improved. Some things are no longer used because they have been replaced with new and better inventions.

Pens and Pencils

Writing tools are always being improved. About 2,500 years ago, feathers and ink were used for writing. Today, we have many choices, including pencils, fountain pens, ballpoint pens, and computers.

Piano Keys

The piano was invented about 300 years ago. Pressing a piano key makes levers move.

Henry Seely, from the United States, invented the electric iron in 1882. He couldn't sell it because hardly anyone had electricity in their homes at that time!

Credit Card

The information on the magnetic strip of a credit card is read by a card reader machine and then sent through a telephone line to a computer.

Microwave Oven

The microwave oven was invented in the 1950s. It uses the effects of electromagnetic radiation. Very short radio waves heat the food and cook it quickly.

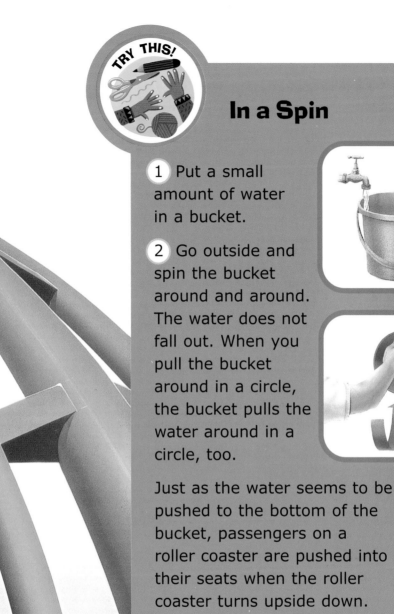

In a Spin

1 Put a small amount of water in a bucket.

1

2 Go outside and spin the bucket around and around. The water does not fall out. When you pull the bucket around in a circle, the bucket pulls the water around in a circle, too.

2

Just as the water seems to be pushed to the bottom of the bucket, passengers on a roller coaster are pushed into their seats when the roller coaster turns upside down.

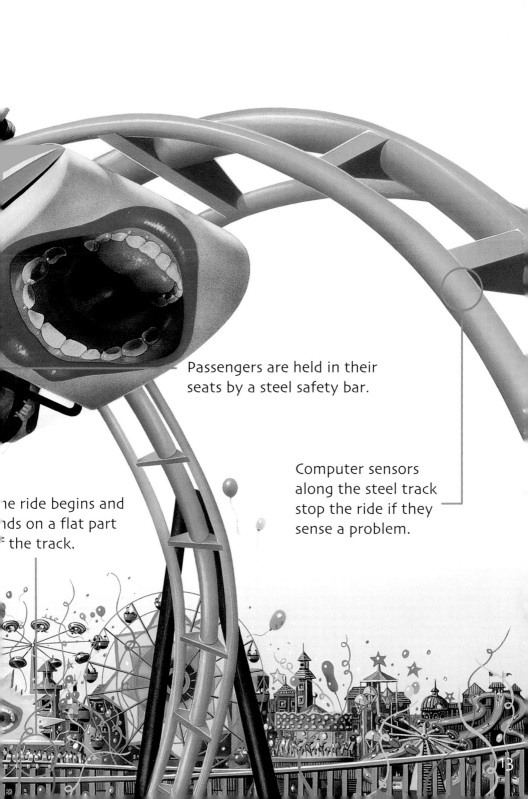

Passengers are held in their seats by a steel safety bar.

Computer sensors along the steel track stop the ride if they sense a problem.

...e ride begins and ...ds on a flat part ...f the track.

A Closer Look

The human eye is an amazing part of the body, but there are many things it cannot see because they are too small or too far away. Special machines have been invented to help people see these objects. Microscopes **magnify** tiny objects. Binoculars let us see over distance. Cameras make pictures that can be kept and enlarged. Telescopes let us study the universe.

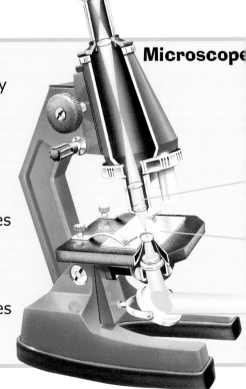

Microscope

• View of a butterfly wing as seen by the human eye

• The same wing magnified 15 times

• The same wing magnified 50 times

Binaculars

The glass lens makes an upside-down picture.

The focusing knob moves the eyepieces closer to or further away from the glass lenses at the front of the binoculars. This makes the image sharp and clear.

1. There are three or more lenses for viewing the object.

2. The object is placed between two pieces of glass.

3. Light is reflected by a tipped mirror.

Each eyepiece has lenses that magnify the image.

Light rays are reflected by glass that turns the image right-side up.

Flying High

Over time, people have thought up many strange inventions to help them fly. They have jumped off high places with large, flapping wings on their arms. They have risen above Earth in hot-air balloons. Today, powerful aircraft fly people around the world using modern **technology**, computer systems, and skilled crews.

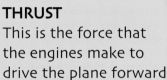

THRUST
This is the force that the engines make to drive the plane forward

A hot-air balloon uses a principle of air pressure. The balloon rises because the hot air inside is lighter than the cooler air outside. The pilot keeps the air inside the balloon hot by using a gas burner for combustion.

LIFT
The plane is pulled upward by the difference in air pressure above and below it.

AERODYNAMICS
An airplane is long and narrow. This shape makes use of the principles of aerodynamics.

SITESEEING • SCIENCE & TECHNOLOGY

What was the first flying machine?

Visit **www.rigbyinfoquest.com**
for more about **FLIGHT.**

Computers and Robots

Computers use **electronic circuits** to store information. Computers control many of the machines we use every day.

Computers are also used to control the most high-tech tools invented so far—robots. Robots can work in places and conditions that are difficult to get to or dangerous. Robots do not get bored doing the same thing every day!

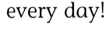

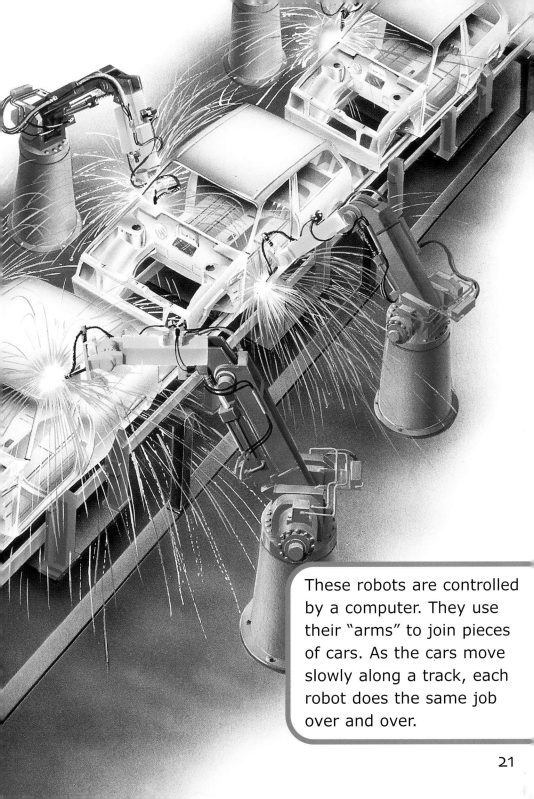

These robots are controlled by a computer. They use their "arms" to join pieces of cars. As the cars move slowly along a track, each robot does the same job over and over.

Virtual Reality

Virtual reality is a new invention that uses computers in a special way. Helmets, gloves, and sensors connect a person's sight, hearing, and touch to a computer. The person can then see the objects as if they really exist. Many virtual reality systems are used in video games. However, athletes, pilots, and other workers also use virtual reality in their training.

This rider can feel the excitement of a ride through Monument Valley, Arizona, in the United States, even though she's not really there. Virtual reality has made it possible to visit places without leaving home.

In September 2001, a tiny robot operated on a patient in France. The robot was controlled by a French surgeon using remote control.

A surprising fact about this operation, however, is that the surgeon was in the United States. The world's first virtual surgery took only 54 minutes and was a complete success.

Will It Work?

Inventing depends on clever and unusual ideas. Trying to predict which inventions will work and how people will like them is never easy. Many famous inventors had ideas that worked and other ideas that might have worked but never happened. Alexander Graham Bell, who invented the telephone, tried to invent a talking fire alarm. Thomas Edison, who invented the lightbulb, also had an idea for underwear that would help people fly!

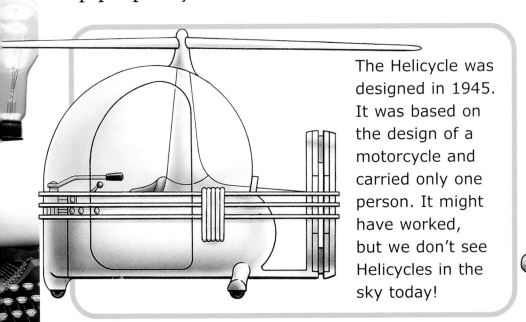

The Helicycle was designed in 1945. It was based on the design of a motorcycle and carried only one person. It might have worked, but we don't see Helicycles in the sky today!

Protecting an Invention

Over the past 500 years, 25 million products, processes, and objects have been invented and patented. Inventors protect their inventions by getting **patents**. Thomas Edison got over 1,000 patents for working inventions. He also got more than 500 patents for things that didn't work!

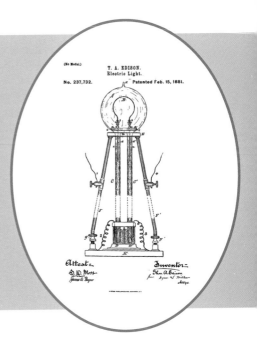

Ice skates with four blades seemed a good idea in 1934. They may have been good for people who couldn't skate on one blade, but they were very difficult to steer.

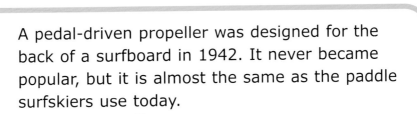

A pedal-driven propeller was designed for the back of a surfboard in 1942. It never became popular, but it is almost the same as the paddle surfskiers use today.

Glossary

electronic circuit – the paths and connections followed by electrons—tiny particles that make up a flow of electricity. Electronic circuits control computers, robots, and modern household devices.

invention – an original, or new, product or process

magnify – to make something look larger than it really is. Instruments such as microscopes and magnifying glasses magnify objects.

patent – an official paper from a government that allows an inventor to be the only one to make or sell a new invention. After 21 years, the invention becomes public property and anyone can make or sell it.

scientific principle – a rule of science that explains how things act. Inventors make use of scientific principles so that their inventions work properly.

technology – the use of science, including new inventions, in everyday life. Technology is used often in the areas of computer science and medicine.

Index

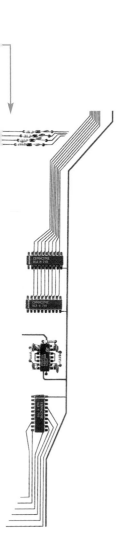

Discussion Starters

1 *Gizmo* is a word that people made up when they couldn't remember the name of a small object. Try making up some other words that could be used instead of *gizmo*.

2 Gravity is a force that pulls things toward the ground. Gravity is strong on Earth but very weak on the moon. How would you have to change things in your home or in your classroom if you moved to the moon?

3 What is your favorite ride at an amusement park? Can you work out which scientific principles explain the forces used in the ride?